KU-153-690

First, I must roll-call my crew members aboard the Starship Crowle. Thanks to my ever-supportive wife, Melanie – The Force Is Always With Her . . . Thanks also to my son, Siôn – an able First Officer, who proves himself to be more heroic than Luke Skywalker. They laugh at (almost all of) my jokes even though, as a writer of comedy, I have Turned To The Dark Side . . .

Thanks to my Mum and Dad, Joan and Ken Crowle, who sit in Mission Control, monitoring 'encouragement' levels.

Back-up crew on Earth includes my ever-smiling expert editor, Jane Richardson, and my always able agent, Sarah Manson.

Thanks to my niece Rachel, who lent me her favourite book on space to read. Thanks also to my brother, Neil, who put his space telescope at my disposal.

Several groups of friends have supported me in my work over the years. These Strange Alien Life Forms include the Kilroy family, the Magee family, the Adams-Jones family, and the Kenvin family. Other total Space Cadets are Carl and Mel Hitchings, Doug and Bev Reynolds, and the Dye-Davies family.

Thanks, finally, to Martin Chatterton, for his illustrations which are truly Out Of This World . . .

Don't forget to flick the top right-hand corner of every page and see me wave!

Check out more fab facts at
know-it-all-guides.co.uk

KNOW-IT-ALL GUIDES

AMAZING SPACE

FAR-OUT FACTS to impress your FRIENDS!

Nigel Crowle

Illustrated by Martin Chatterton

PUFFIN BOOKS

Published by the Penguin Group
Penguin Books Ltd, 80 Strand, London WC2R 0RL, England
Penguin Group (USA) Inc., 375 Hudson Street, New York, New York 10014, USA
Penguin Group (Canada), 90 Eglinton Avenue East, Suite 700, Toronto, Ontario,
Canada M4P 2Y3 (a division of Pearson Penguin Canada Inc.)
Penguin Ireland, 25 St Stephen's Green, Dublin 2, Ireland (a division of
Penguin Books Ltd)
Penguin Group (Australia), 250 Camberwell Road, Camberwell, Victoria 3124,
Australia
(a division of Pearson Australia Group Pty Ltd)
Penguin Books India Pvt Ltd, 11 Community Centre, Panchsheel Park,
New Delhi – 110 017, India
Penguin Group (NZ), 67 Apollo Drive, Mairangi Bay, Auckland 1310,
New Zealand (a division of Pearson New Zealand Ltd)
Penguin Books (South Africa) (Pty) Ltd, 24 Sturdee Avenue, Rosebank,
Johannesburg 2196, South Africa

Penguin Books Ltd, Registered Offices: 80 Strand, London WC2R 0RL, England

penguin.com

First published 2007
1

Text copyright © Nigel Crowle, 2007
Illustrations copyright © Martin Chatterton, 2007
All rights reserved

The moral right of the author and illustrator has been asserted

Set in Bookman Old Style
Made and printed in England by Clays Ltd, St Ives plc

Except in the United States of America, this book is sold subject to the condition
that it shall not, by way of trade or otherwise, be lent, re-sold, hired out, or otherwise
circulated without the publisher's prior consent in any form of binding or cover other
than that in which it is published and without a similar condition including this
condition being imposed on the subsequent purchaser

British Library Cataloguing in Publication Data
A CIP catalogue record for this book is available from the British Library

ISBN-13: 978-0-141-32072-4
ISBN-10: 0-141-32072-9

Llyfrgelloed Bwrdeistref Sirol
Rhondda-Cynon-Taf
Rhondda-Cynon-Taff
County Borough Libraries

Contents

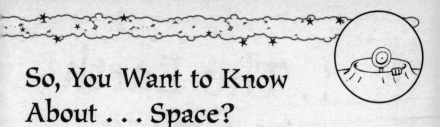

So, You Want to Know About . . . Space?

Space is a pretty big place. It stretches on for . . . well . . . we don't really know how far. When we look up into the sky at night, some galaxies are so far away from us that they contain stars whose light has taken almost 13 billion years to reach us on Earth. And yet we have only explored one miniscule corner of the universe.

But we're learning new things about space all the time – from rockets and satellites, to planets and stars. If we keep putting those fantastic facts together, one day you could end up with a book the size of a planet! How amazing is *that*?

But be warned! As you explore space with the help of this book, you must try to keep your wits about you down here on Earth.

That's because some of the following facts are totally made up, deviously created to try and trick you. Can you sort the truth from the space junk and Find That Fib in every chapter? Your fact-sorting space mission begins here. Good luck!

1. The Earth in Space

As they say at the start of each edition of *Star Trek*, space really is the final frontier. What's more, we have only just begun to explore it. So, let's make a start by Finding Those Fibs!

Where is Space?

The Earth is surrounded by the **atmosphere**, an envelope of gases that allows us to breathe. Space starts where the atmosphere ends . . . except you can't actually see it! Most passenger aircraft cruise about **9 km above Earth** but you'd need to travel much further out to reach space. You'd still find traces of those atmospheric gases even **160 km above the Earth**.

Most scientists claim that space begins **100 km above the Earth**. Flight engineers are a bit more exact, though – they reckon that space starts at the point at which you can see a spacecraft starting to heat up as it re-enters our Earth's atmosphere. That's about **122 km above Earth**, and they call this the entry interface.

And, finally, major space powers talk about space beginning at 'the point in any orbit nearest to the body being orbited'. An orbit is the path followed by an object in space as it goes around another object.

Quickie Quiz

If you are still confused about where space begins, you could ask an official organization . . . but which one? Is it:

a) **The National Association of School Caretakers and Dinner Ladies?**

b) **The Martian Space Evaluation Body?**

c) **The United Nations Office for Outer Space Affairs?**

*The answer's c). The only organization which can actually define where space begins is the **United Nations Office for Outer Space Affairs** in Vienna. However, even they can't decide, and their official line is: 'There is no agreement on the limit of outer space.' Hope that's cleared things up for you . . .*

Even with today's clever technology, we still can't get **enough speed** to travel across our own Solar System. An object like Pluto, for instance, orbits 5,913,520,000 km from the Sun. NASA has worked out that if we left Earth for Pluto in 2006, we still wouldn't reach anywhere near there until 2014 to 2016.

Top Ten Brightest Stars Seen from Planet Earth

10. Sirius
9. Canopus
8. Rigil Kentasaurus
7. Arcturus
6. Vega
5. Capella
4. Rigel
3. Procyon
2. Betelgeuse
1. The Sun (yes, the Sun actually is a star!)

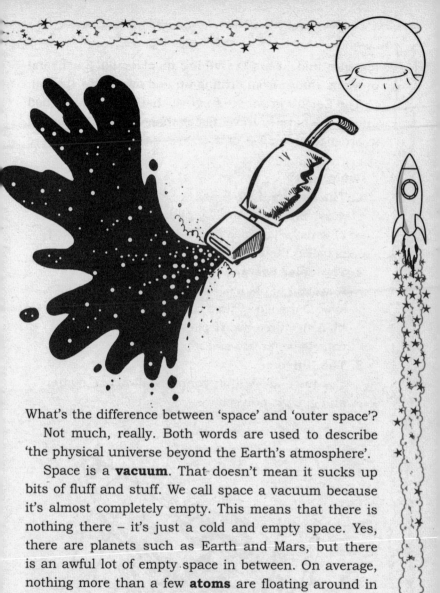

What's the difference between 'space' and 'outer space'?

Not much, really. Both words are used to describe 'the physical universe beyond the Earth's atmosphere'.

Space is a **vacuum**. That doesn't mean it sucks up bits of fluff and stuff. We call space a vacuum because it's almost completely empty. This means that there is nothing there – it's just a cold and empty space. Yes, there are planets such as Earth and Mars, but there is an awful lot of empty space in between. On average, nothing more than a few **atoms** are floating around in every cubic metre in space, atom being the smallest, simplest form of matter.

The vacuum in space is created by the pull of **gravity** – the force of attraction that makes matter clump together and keeps everything in place on Earth and prevents things from drifting up and away into space.

The Earth's gravity is so great that rockets launched into space have to travel faster than 11 km per second in order to break free of it.

What is It?
1. The Galaxy
A system of about 100 billion stars. There are billions of galaxies in the universe. Our galaxy is called the Milky Way.
2. The Solar System
A system of planets and other bodies orbiting a star. Our solar system consists of the Sun, eight planets, three dwarf planets, over 100 moons, comets, asteroids and more!
3. The Universe
The huge space that contains all of the matter and energy in existence.

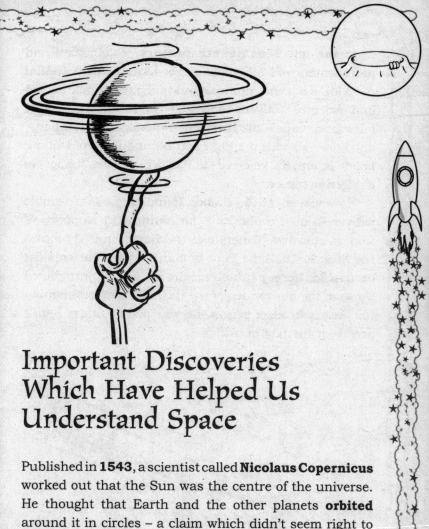

Important Discoveries Which Have Helped Us Understand Space

Published in **1543**, a scientist called **Nicolaus Copernicus** worked out that the Sun was the centre of the universe. He thought that Earth and the other planets **orbited** around it in circles – a claim which didn't seem right to other astronomers.

Between **1609** and **1621**, German scientist **Johannes Kepler** worked out that the planets orbiting the Sun travelled in **ellipses** – or squashed circles. He also realized that the strong pull of attraction between the Earth and Moon, together with the pull of the Sun, causes **tides** to swash in and out on Earth.

In **the mid seventeenth century**, Italian physicist, astronomer, and all-round clever-clogs **Galileo Galilei** did a lot to advance our knowledge of physics, astronomy and science. Galileo suggested improvements to the telescope, made a number of astronomical observations, and came up with the First and Second Laws of Motion. Later scientists referred to Galileo as the 'father of modern astronomy'.

However, in 1616, Galileo found himself in trouble with religious authorities for writing in support of Copernicus that planets like the Earth orbited around the Sun. In 1632 the Pope demanded that Galileo went on trial for **heresy** (which means his views contradicted those of the authorities of the day). He was found guilty too, but instead of prison, he was placed under house arrest for the rest of his life.

It wasn't all bad, though. At least Galileo also gets a namecheck in **Queen's** rock-tastic number-one hit single 'Bohemian Rhapsody'. (Just before the headbanging instrumental bit . . .)

In **1687**, **Isaac Newton** published his *Law of Universal Gravitation*. This explained that any heavenly body attracts every other body because of its mass. **The bigger the body, the bigger the force of gravity**, which holds together everything that makes up our universe. The largest star in our universe, the Sun, reaches out trillions of kilometres into space, and keeps the planets in orbit.

Space shuttles never leave **Earth's orbit** – they travel around Earth nearly **320 km** above its surface, moving at about 25 km per second. That's roughly seven or eight times faster than the fastest aeroplane. If you were travelling on-board a space shuttle, it would take you approximately eight and a half minutes after lift-off to reach that speed.

German scientist **Albert Einstein** came up with some startling evidence in his *Theory of Relativity* in **1915**. He proved that nothing can move faster than the **speed of light**. This is measured at 300,000 km per second.

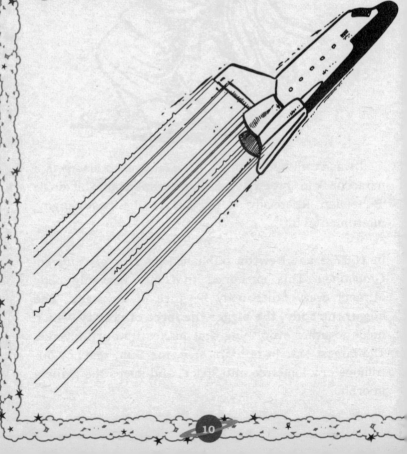

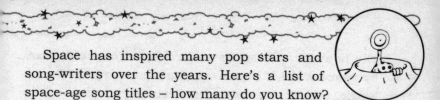

Space has inspired many pop stars and song-writers over the years. Here's a list of space-age song titles – how many do you know?

Top Space-Age Song Titles of the Last Ten Years
'Sun Hits the Sky' (Supergrass, 1997)
'Stars' (Roxette, 1999)
'Dancing in the Moonlight' (Toploader, 2001)
'Star 69' (Fatboy Slim, 2001)
'Venus and Mars' (Jo Breezer, 2001)
'Space Walk' (Lemon Jelly, 2001)
'Mercury' (Lowgold, 2001)
'Full Moon' (Brandy, 2002)
'Dream Universe' (DJ Garry, 2002)
'Heaven is a Place on Earth' (Soda Club, 2003)
'Girl in the Moon' (Darius, 2003)
'Total Eclipse of the Heart' (Jan Wayne, 2003)
'Walking in the Sun' (Travis, 2004)
'Satellite of Love 04' (Lou Reed, 2004)
'Wishing on a Star' (Paul Weller, 2004)
'Heaven and Earth' (Pop, 2004)
'Staring at the Sun' (Rooster, 2005)
'Rocket – A Natural Gambler'
     (Braund Reynolds, 2005)
'Falling Stars' (Sunset Strippers, 2005)
'When the Sun Goes Down' (Arctic Monkeys, 2006)

The pop star who seems to have been most **obsessed by space** when it comes to writing pop songs is **David Bowie**. (Ask your mum and dad who he is . . .)

Here are **Bowie's Top Five Space Hits**, which are still favourites on the airwaves today:

'Space Oddity' (1969, 1975)
'Starman' (1972)
'Life on Mars?' (1973)
'Loving the Alien' (1985, 2002)
'Hello, Spaceboy' (1996)

Groovy Galaxies

There are actually three types of **galaxies** in space. These are:

Spiral

Elliptical (oval-shaped – the most popular type of galaxy)

Irregular

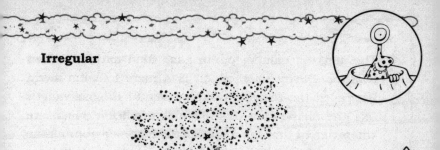

Our own **Milky Way** is a spiral galaxy. If you look up at the night sky during summer in the northern hemisphere, you can see the Milky Way – it's a faint band of stars stretching over the sky.

Quickie Quiz

Even travelling at the speed of light, how long would it take to cross the galaxy from edge to edge? Is it:

a) Over 100 minutes?

b) Over 100,000 years?

c) Never?

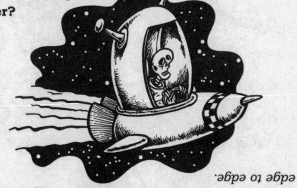

The answer's b). Even travelling at the speed of light, it would take over 100,000 years to cross the galaxy from edge to edge.

The nearest galaxy to ours is the **Dustbin Galaxy** (*Galaxia Dustybinus*), which is a mere 878 km away. It's called the Dustbin Galaxy because it looks exactly like the shape of a dustbin (not a wheelie bin . . .), when viewed through a space telescope. It's appropriate because this galaxy is completely composed of large dust particles swirling through space.

Top Four Names of Sweets or Chocolate Bars Inspired by Space

4. **Galaxy**
3. **Milky Way**
2. **Starbursts**
1. **Mars**

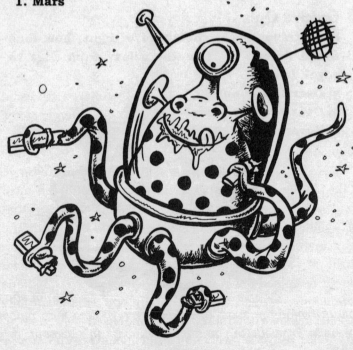

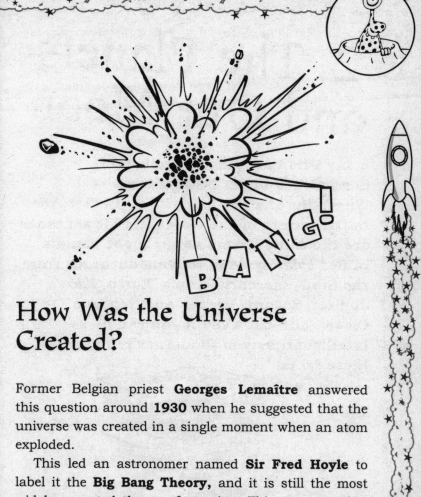

How Was the Universe Created?

Former Belgian priest **Georges Lemaître** answered this question around **1930** when he suggested that the universe was created in a single moment when an atom exploded.

This led an astronomer named **Sir Fred Hoyle** to label it the **Big Bang Theory,** and it is still the most widely accepted theory of creation. This suggests that 15 billion years ago, a massive explosion occurred. The universe expanded from nothing to 2 billion billion km wide in a single second. Matter scattered everywhere, and this cooled down from trillions of degrees to billions of degrees – which was still totally hot! This eventually cooled down a lot more, then condensed over time to form our universe, with its planets, galaxies and stars.

2. The Planets and Our Moon

Many Vile Earthlings Munch Jam Sandwiches Under Newspapers.
What? No, it's not a mistake. In fact, the initial letters of the words in that sentence are the same letters as the eight planets in our solar system, moving outwards from the Sun – Mercury, Venus, Earth, Mars, Jupiter, Saturn, Uranus and Neptune. Clever, eh? Let's see if you can be as intelligent, as you Find That Fib amongst these facts!

The planets are divided into two groups. The **four closest to the Sun** are called **terrestrial**, from the Latin word for 'land'. This is because they are small, dense and have hard surfaces. These rocky planets are Earth, Mercury, Venus and Mars.

The four outer planets beyond Mars are called **Jovian** because they all look like Jupiter. These giant outer planets are mainly composed of gases and are Jupiter, Saturn, Uranus and Neptune.

Mercury Fact File

- Mercury is approximately **4,880 km** in diameter.
- Like Earth and Venus, Mercury is rocky and has an **iron core** with a radius of 1,800 to 1,900 km. However, Mercury's core extends three quarters of the way to the surface of the planet.
- Mercury has a **very thin atmosphere** as a planet. Atoms are continually being blasted off its surface by an intense solar wind.

Quickie Quiz

As the closest planet to the Sun, Mercury is also the fastest-moving planet in the solar system. So, how long does it take to orbit around the Sun? Is it:

a) just 8.8 seconds?

b) just 88 days?

c) just 888 years?

The answer's b). Mercury takes just 88 days to orbit the Sun, and has an average orbiting speed of 172,248 km per hour.

Venus Fact File

- Venus is the **second planet** from the Sun and the **sixth largest**.
- Venus's **orbit** is the most **circular** of that of any planet, and is **108,200,000 km** from the Sun.
- Apart from the Sun and Moon, it is the **brightest** object in the sky.
- With a diameter of **12,104 km**, Venus is almost the same size as Earth but you wouldn't want to live there – nor would you be able to! Not only is the atmosphere made up of carbon dioxide, it's surrounded by thick clouds of sulphuric acid, and the planet itself is roasting hot and covered in active volcanoes. Venus's surface temperature is hot enough to melt lead.
- Venus is well known to scientists, who have gathered more information about the surface of Venus than the seabed of planet Earth. For example, they know that Venus once had large amounts of water like Earth, but now is quite dry. This is probably due to an extreme 'greenhouse effect'. The Sun's radiation passed through the dense clouds surrounding the planet, but – as Venus's surface heated up – it couldn't escape. So the heat was trapped by Venus's atmosphere and the water boiled away.
- On **8 June 2004**, Venus passed directly between the Earth and the Sun, appearing as a large black dot travelling across the Sun's disk. This rare event is known as a '**transit of Venus**' and the last time it took place was in 1882. The next transit of Venus is due in 2012, but after that you'll have to wait until 2117.

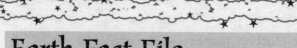

Earth Fact File

- It is the **fifth largest** planet.
- Earth has a diameter of **12,753 km**.
- It is a minimum distance away from the Sun of **149,503 million km**. Its maximum distance from the Sun is **152 million km**.
- Earth is the only planet whose name doesn't come from Roman or Greek mythology.
- Earth is the **densest planet** in the solar system. As a whole, Earth is made up of the following elements:
  34.6% Iron
  29.5% Oxygen
  15.2% Silicon
  12.7% Magnesium
  2.4% Nickel
  1.9% Sulphur
  0.05% Titanium

- 71 per cent of the Earth's surface is covered with water, and it's the only planet upon which water can exist in liquid form on the surface. Liquid water is essential for life as we know it.
- Earth's atmosphere is made up of 78 per cent nitrogen, 21 per cent oxygen, and traces of argon, carbon dioxide and water, with a few other gases.
- The coldest temperature ever measured on planet Earth was 89 degrees Celsius at Vostok, Antarctica, on **21 July 1983**.

Top Three Hottest Places on Planet Earth

1. **Death Valley**, California, recorded a temperature of 56.7 degrees Celsius on 10 July 1913.
2. **El Azizia** in Libya recorded a temperature of 57.8 degrees Celsius on 13 September 1922 – the hottest ever measured.
3. Ethiopia's **Dallol** in the Danakil Depression lies so much below sea level that temperatures have unofficially reached as high as 63 degrees Celsius.

The Moon Fact File

- The Moon is the Earth's only **natural satellite**. (A 'satellite' is anything that orbits something else in space.) The Moon orbits the Earth about **384,000 km** away.
- As the Moon moves, the constantly changing angle means light from the Sun creates **different phases**, or shapes (see our handy guide below).
- It has a diameter of **3,476 km**, and is the only astral body apart from Earth to have been visited by humans.
- Most rocks on the surface of the Moon seem to be between 3 and 4.6 billion years old.
- During the *Apollo* and *Luna* missions, astronauts brought **381 kg** of **Moon rock** back home to Earth. According to NASA scientists, Moon rock differs from Earth rocks because it contains **particles of glass** produced over 3 billion years ago by explosive volcanoes and meteorite impacts. Also, the *Apollo* Moon rocks are peppered with what astronauts nicknamed '**zap pits**'. These are tiny craters from

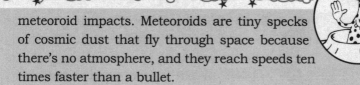

meteoroid impacts. Meteoroids are tiny specks of cosmic dust that fly through space because there's no atmosphere, and they reach speeds ten times faster than a bullet.

The Different Phases of the Moon

New Moon The Moon's unlit side faces the Earth. The Moon is not visible.

Waxing Crescent The Moon appears to be partly but less than one half lit up by direct sunlight. The small part of the Moon's disk that is lit up is increasing.

First Quarter One half of the Moon appears to be lit up by direct sunlight. The small part of the Moon's disk that is illuminated is increasing.

Waxing Gibbous The Moon appears to be more than one half but not fully lit by direct sunlight. The fraction of the Moon's disk that is lit is increasing.

Full Moon The Moon's illuminated side faces the Earth. The Moon appears to be completely lit by direct sunlight.

Waning Gibbous The Moon seems to be more than one half but not fully lit by direct sunlight. The small part of the Moon's disk that is lit is decreasing.

Last Quarter One half of the Moon appears to be lit by direct sunlight. The small part of the Moon's disk that is lit up is decreasing.

Waning Crescent The Moon appears to be partly but less than one half lit by direct sunlight. The small part of the Moon's disk that is illuminated is getting smaller.

Mars Fact File

- It's the **fourth planet** from the Sun and the **seventh largest** in our solar system.
- The **Red Planet** is about half the size of Earth, with a diameter of **6,794 km**.
- It has an orbit of **227,940,000 km** from the Sun.
- With temperatures ranging from -133 degrees Celsius in winter up to 27 degrees in summer, definite seasons and even ice caps at the poles, Mars is the planet **most similar to Earth** and therefore most likely to support life. In July 2005, the European Space Agency probe, the *Mars Express*, took a photograph of a patch of **water** 35 km wide on the floor of a crater. Scientists were very excited by this discovery as the presence of

water indicates that some form of primitive life is probable. But Mars's atmosphere is actually very thin and mainly made up of carbon dioxide, so it's unlikely that there is any **life as we know it** on Mars.

Back in **1877**, **Giovanni Schiaparelli** first spotted what seemed to be **deep channels** on Mars. This led other astronomers to wrongly suppose that there was a race of Martians digging these canals to water farmland. These canyons are at least 6 km deep in some places.

The **Olympus Mons** volcano is the **largest of four volcanoes** near Mars's equator. It last erupted around 25 million years ago, and – at 25 km high – is three times higher than Mount Everest.

In **August 2003**, Mars blazed really brightly in the sky, **glowing** like a red, burning coal as it came closer than usual to our planet – but still more than 55 million km away! The last time Mars shone that brilliantly, our planet was freezing and our cavemen and women ancestors could only stay warm by huddling around camp fires. That was during the last Ice Age nearly 60,000 years ago.

Jupiter Fact File

- Jupiter is the **fifth planet** from the Sun.
- With a diameter of **143,000 km**, it is more than **twice as large** as all the other planets combined. In fact, the mass of Jupiter is 318 times that of Earth.
- It has an orbit that is **778,330,000 km** from the Sun.

Like Saturn, Jupiter is primarily a gas or Jovian planet. Although it probably has a rocky core, it doesn't have a solid surface, being made up of liquid hydrogen and a swirling atmosphere of helium and hydrogen gas. That's why, despite being the largest planet, it's still so light that it would **float in water** . . . provided you could find a bowl that's big enough!

Named after the king of the **Roman gods**, Jupiter has thirty-nine moons circling around it – and all except one (Amalthea) are named after the many **lovers of Zeus**, according to Roman mythology.

Saturn Fact File

- Saturn is the **sixth planet** from the Sun.
- It is the second largest, with a diameter of **120,536 km**.
- It has an orbit of **1,429,400,000 km** from the Sun.
- The planets Jupiter, Neptune and Uranus all have 'rings' around them, but Saturn's are the most impressive. There are **three rings** visible from Earth, made up of chunks of mainly ice and rock orbiting around Saturn at great speed – some as small as a sand grain, others as big as a bus.
- Saturn's rings are highly visible because the ice

reflects Sunlight, just as ice does on a winter's day on Earth.

- The planet's rings are actually made up of about 10,000 small rings, called ringlets. The average ring is about 280,000 km across, but less than 1 km thick. Yet Saturn is so huge in size, the rings appear paper-thin.

Uranus Fact File

- Uranus is the **seventh planet** from the Sun.
- It is the **third largest** planet in the solar system, and has at least twenty-one named moons and six unnamed ones.
- At **51,118 km**, Uranus is larger in diameter but smaller in mass than Neptune.
- It has an orbit that is **2,870,990,000 km** from the Sun.
- Uranus's **blue-green colour** is the result of light being absorbed by the layer of methane gas in its upper atmosphere.
- Uranus may have been the sort of planet name that has made generations of schoolchildren giggle, but it could've been worse. It could've been called the planet **Tinkerbell**. Uranus was discovered in 1781 by a former musician, **William Herschel**. He had trained his telescope towards space and his pet cat knocked against it, swinging it around. Herschel looked through the re-positioned telescope to find Uranus. Once he'd made his accidental discovery, Herschel originally wanted to call the planet Tinkerbell, after his cat.

Neptune Fact File

- Neptune is the **eighth planet** from the Sun.
- It is the **fourth largest** planet, with a diameter of **49,532 km** which makes Neptune smaller in diameter – but larger in mass – than Uranus.
- Neptune's orbit is 4,504,000,000 km from the Sun.
- Neptune lies 1.6 billion km beyond Uranus.
- In Roman mythology, Neptune was the **god of the sea**, and that's why it has the nickname of the **Blue Planet**. Its colour is a mystery to scientists who haven't yet worked out which chemical compound gives it such a rich blue hue, although methane clearly contributes to the colour. Reaching temperatures as low as **200 degrees below zero**, it's cold on Neptune!

- Measuring **2,706 km** across, **Triton** is the largest of Neptune's eleven moons.
- Like Pluto, it's a deep-frozen world and the moon is covered with frozen nitrogen and methane, together with geysers which blow out clouds of nitrogen gas and dust. It also has the lowest recorded surface temperature in the solar system, at a blisteringly cold **-235 degrees Celsius**. It's so cold that when the gas nitrogen freezes on the surface, it actually turns into a kind of pink snow.

Dwarf Planet Fact File

Pluto

- Spare a thought for Pluto, which is **no longer officially a planet** in our solar system. 76 years after it was discovered by American Clyde Tombaugh, Pluto has been stripped of its status. In 2006, 2,500 experts voted against keeping Pluto as a planet. Some astronomers have argued for years that Pluto should never have been thought of as a planet. Now they've been proved right and it isn't!

- Pluto was named by a **schoolgirl**. In March 1930, 11-year-old Venetia Burnley from Oxford had been told by her grandfather that a new planet had been discovered. She immediately suggested that it be called 'Pluto' as she knew that most planets were named after mythological figures. In addition, Pluto had the same initial letters as Dr Percy Lowell, a scientist who had maintained for many years that such a planet existed. Young Venetia went on to become a teacher.

Four Reasons Why Scientists Don't Think Pluto is a Planet

1. Pluto isn't really big enough to be a planet at all. Measuring a mere **2,274 km** in diameter, it's tinier than our own Moon.

2. Unlike all the other planets, Pluto seems to be a dense mass of **rock and ice**.

3. In appearance, it seems to be a **giant comet**, coming from an area rich in comets called the Kuiper Belt.

4. It has that **strange orbit** that differs from the other major planets, because it is far less circular – in fact, it's positively eccentric – as it travels around the Sun.

Other Large Objects in Space

At the same conference that rejected Pluto, scientists refused to accept planetary status for **2003 UB313**, which had been discovered moving across the sky beyond Neptune. This object – larger than Pluto – is a typical member of the Kuiper Belt, but astronomers prefer to call it a 'Trans-Neptunian', rather than a planet. It's actually 3,000 km in diameter.

Currently about 97 times further from the Sun than the Earth, it's the farthest-known object in the solar system.

The name 2003 UB313 doesn't seem to be catching on as scientists also refer to it under the following nicknames:

Xena
Santa
Rudolph
Easterbunny
and the **Flying Dutchman**.

The other two known dwarf planets in our solar system are Ceres at 950 km in diameter and Eris, which is 2,400 km across.

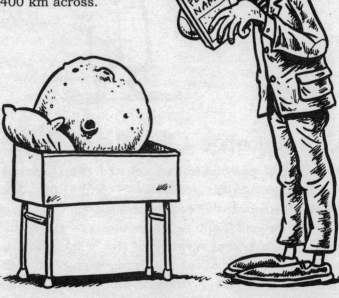

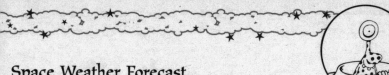

Space Weather Forecast

Hello, and if you feel like visiting the planets in the inner solar system, here is the weather.

It's hot, hot, hot on Venus — an average 480 degrees Celsius on the surface — but clouds will block out a lot of the sunlight.

On fast-moving Mercury, you can look forward to temperatures varying wildly. They'll be a baking hot 450 degrees Celsius during the day, before dropping to -180 degrees Celsius at night.

Further away in the solar system, no danger of rain on Mars. However, zip up your anoraks and tie your scarves tightly, because the winds blowing across the surface of the good old Red Planet can reach up to 300 km per hour, whipping up a fine old dust storm.

Finally, back here on Earth, it's rain, rain and more rain, I'm afraid. That's all the weather news. Back in a moment with sports news, on the day that Asteroids United went down 5—nil to Uranus Wanderers . . .

3. Lost in Space

There's a lot of dangerous rubbish floating about in the solar system – as you'll find out if you read on. Oh, and don't forget to try and Spot the Fib in this chapter – that really *is* rubbish.

In **1999**, US Space Command reckoned that there is around 1,800,000 kg of **junk** or man-made debris bobbing around in space. If each object measured only one centimetre, that's about 110,000 items. However, each of those pieces of junk is big enough to damage space equipment such as a telescope, or a satellite. A tiny **speck of paint** that had flaked off from a satellite once dug a pit in a space-shuttle window over half a centimetre wide! Because it had built up so much speed travelling across the vacuum of space, the paint particle hit the shuttle with the force of a **bowling ball** travelling at a speedy 112 km per hour.

Scientists need to keep a close eye on all this space junk as they could be deadly to a space mission.

As of **21 June 2000**, scientists had counted **8,927** man-made objects floating in space. They were:

2,671 satellites (working or not)

6,096 chunks of rubbish

90 space probes

Russia's *Mir* space station released almost **200** bin bags during the first ten years it circled the Earth.

When a spacecraft breaks up, this can also generate a lot of rubbish. In **1996** when the upper part of a *Pegasus* rocket disintegrated, the explosion generated a cloud of around **300,000 fragments**, each around four millimetres in size.

Scientists at NASA's Orbital Debris Program are responsible for tracking space junk. Since 1958, almost **17,000 objects** re-entered the Earth's atmosphere.

But on average only about seventy a year fall to Earth.

Now, with all these objects whizzing around, you might be wondering **how likely is it that a piece of junk will fall from space and hit you on the head?** Don't worry, it's *very* unlikely. Most bits of space junk burn up on re-entry, or land in seas since three quarters of our planet is covered in water. You are most likely to get hit by space junk if you are at an altitude between 800 to 1,000 km above Earth. That's because that area not only has the greatest concentration of objects that have been launched into space, but also has been the site of several explosions.

Quickie Quiz

Have you ever wondered what is the oldest piece of debris or junk still in orbit? Here are some suggestions. Is it:

a) A bit of a Russian satellite?
b) The whole of a US satellite?
c) A teddy bear left on the Moon by *Apollo 12* astronauts?

*The answer is **b**. Vanguard 1 was the name given to the second US satellite and was launched in March 1958. It only worked properly for six years.*

In **1965**, American astronauts made their first **spacewalk**, and astronaut **Edward White** lost a glove which floated off across the universe. The glove stayed in orbit for a month, reaching speeds of up to 28,000 km per hour and becoming the most dangerous item of clothing in history!

The ***Skylab*** was the most spectacular piece of space junk to re-enter the Earth's atmosphere. The Americans launched *Skylab* in **1973**, two years after Russia led the way with the first orbiting space station. However, six years later, the US space station came splashing home. One bit landed in the Indian Ocean and another chunk of junk ended up in Australia.

In **1969**, *Apollo 12* astronauts **Pete Conrad** and **Al Bean** were astonished to look out of their spacecraft window and see a small chunk of **chocolate-chip cookie** floating around in space. They collected it and took it back to

Houston Space Control who confirmed that the cookie was part of rations from an earlier Apollo mission, when it had been spat out by astronaut **Buzz Aldrin** who didn't like chocolate flavour and preferred peanut butter.

In **May 2005**, *Science* magazine reported that millions of tons of **dandruff** are circling Earth, blocking out sunlight, causing rain and spreading disease. It seems that vast clouds of **fine dust** in the atmosphere are made up of bits of decaying leaves, animal hair, dead human skin and dandruff. US scientist **Dr Gene Shinn** reckons that this dust might explain why more and more people around the world are starting to suffer from **asthma**.

4. Strange Space Happenings

You've been told some pretty strange things about space so far. But if it's weirdness you want, then listen to this selection of hard-to-believe stories. Can you Find That Fib in this lot?

Fake Moon Landings

Six per cent of Americans seem to think that all the pictures of *Apollo* astronauts landing on the Moon on **20 July 1969** were faked and that man has never landed on the Moon! Here are three of the questions they claim they need answering, and the answers:

1. Why don't we see stars, just black sky, in the pictures of Moon landings?
If you took a photo outside on Earth on the darkest night ever, and you used the same camera settings as the astronauts, you wouldn't see stars either. A camera on a fast-shutter exposure isn't able to pick out the stars on a black background. They are still there – they're just faint, that's all. Furthermore, the sky always looks black due to the fact that there is no atmosphere on the Moon.

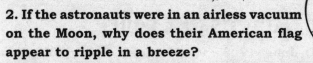

2. If the astronauts were in an airless vacuum on the Moon, why does their American flag appear to ripple in a breeze?

A flag can wave in a vacuum – provided an astronaut jiggles it. If the astronaut is inserting the flagpole into the ground, as he is in the famous pictures, he rotates it. The pole moves first and the cloth will follow. And so this isn't air that is moving the flag, it is actually the astronaut.

3. As the rockets land on the Moon, dust gets blown away, so why can we clearly see astronauts' footprints in dust that's only a few metres from the rocket?

The only dust that would have been blown around by the exhaust blast of the *Apollo* rocket was the dust physically touched by that exhaust, or dust moved by other bits of flying dust. Only the dust directly under or close to the rocket was blown out by the exhaust.

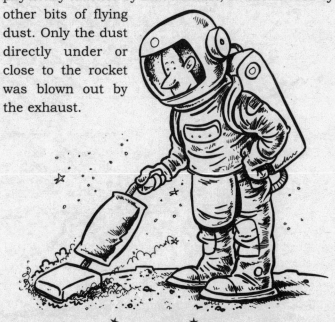

The Tunguska Event

On **30 June 1908**, near **Siberia's Stony Tunguska River**, something strange happened. A **huge fireball**, nearly as bright as the Sun, moved across the sky. Minutes later, bystanders were blown off their feet by a shock wave that broke windows up to 650 km away. Also, a 2,100 sq. km area of trees was scorched and knocked flat – apart from a few trees in the centre which were still weirdly upright, although stripped of bark and branches. How could this happen?

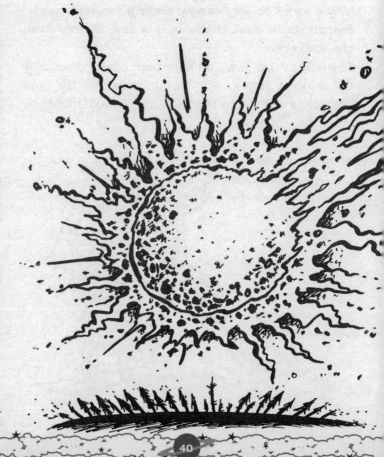

Some scientists think what came to be known as the Tunguska Event was due to a **stony meteorite** bursting through the atmosphere at high speed

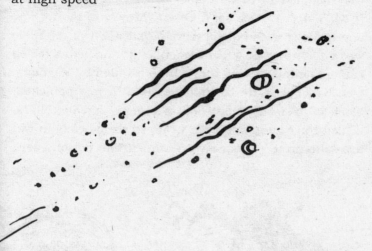

and exploding 6 km above the ground. The effect was similar to a huge **atomic bomb**. However, don't panic, as scientists reckon that such events are only likely to happen once every 300 years.

The other possibility is the Tunguska Event was caused by a **comet,** a huge ball of ice and dirt (see page 68 for more on comets). A comet would have been turned to vapour upon hitting the Earth's atmosphere, and the dust would have hung around in the upper atmosphere, which might explain why the skies glowed for days after the impact.

Or, spookily, could the whole thing have been a simple result of **UFO activity** – like an alien spaceship exploding? We still don't know for sure.

The War of the Worlds

On **30 October 1938**, millions of Americans thought the USA had been **invaded** by **Martian** monsters as they listened to their radios. Orson Welles had taken H. G. Wells's classic sci-fi novel, *The War of the Worlds*, and made it sound like a news broadcast. Dance music was interrupted by fake news bulletins and actors fooled listeners into believing they'd been invaded by Martians, who had begun destroying the USA. People panicked, blocked roads as they tried to escape, hid in cellars, loaded their guns and even wrapped their heads in wet towels to protect themselves from Martian poison gas!

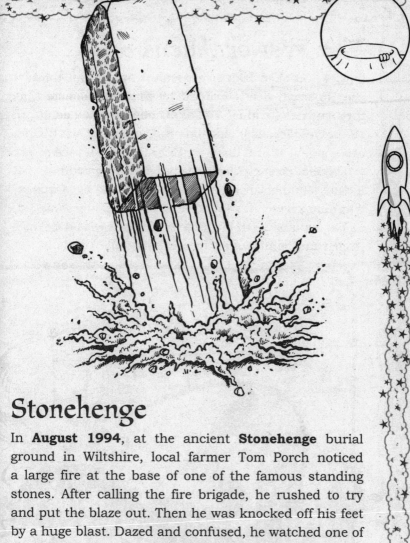

Stonehenge

In **August 1994**, at the ancient **Stonehenge** burial ground in Wiltshire, local farmer Tom Porch noticed a large fire at the base of one of the famous standing stones. After calling the fire brigade, he rushed to try and put the blaze out. Then he was knocked off his feet by a huge blast. Dazed and confused, he watched one of the huge stone blocks rocketing skywards. There were no scorch marks on the grass and a few minutes later the **stone spacecraft** returned, and hovered cautiously before landing back in its original position. Farmer Porch had a few problems convincing firemen and police that he'd seen a stone spaceship!

The Roswell Aliens

In **1947** an alien craft supposedly crashed in the desert near Roswell, New Mexico. Eyewitnesses claimed that they saw dead and injured **alien bodies** being captured by the military, who also took the spacecraft to an Ohio base.

Did the 'Roswell Incident' ever really happen?

No, say the US government, who've always denied that aliens were ever found at Roswell.

Yes, said newspapers, who – at the time of the crash – reported the hiding away of a 'flying disk'.

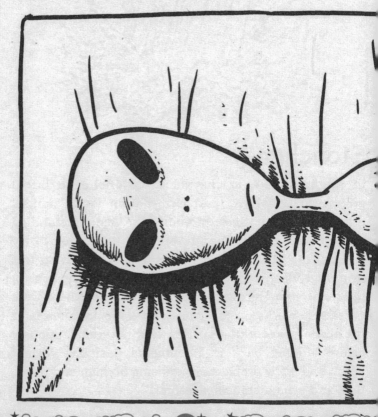

And yes, said the eyewitnesses, who also saw the film footage showing medical experiments being carried out upon the aliens who looked like little humans with big eyes!

Now, if that last point sounds familiar, it's probably because you've seen *Alien Autopsy*, a 2006 movie about faking . . . well, an alien autopsy, and starring Ant McPartlin and Declan Donnelly, more commonly known as Ant 'n' Dec.

So, the Roswell film footage might have been faked, but what about the reports of a flying saucer? If an incident *did* happen at Roswell, it's most likely that it was all

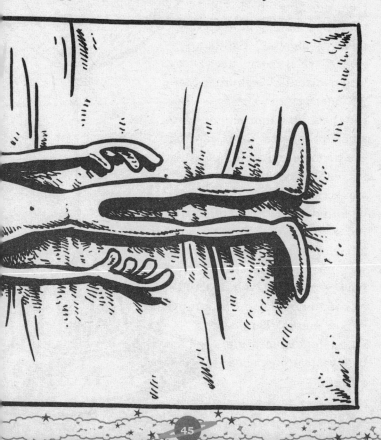

part of a top-secret government experiment involving weather balloons. Some think that they were sent into the air to detect Soviet nuclear bombs.

Scottish UFOs

One morning in 1979, while dog walking in woods near Livingston, Scotland, Bob Taylor came across a **large circular sphere**, about 20 metres in size. As Bob watched in amazement, two smaller spheres dropped from the metallic machine, and their spikes attached themselves to his trousers. As Bob's dog barked, he found himself pulled towards the strange craft. Next thing he knew, a bruised Bob woke up, with torn trousers and the craft having vanished. Was it a UFO? Nobody knows . . . but strange rocket marks really were found in the clearing by investigating police officers.

Pembrokeshire Triangle

One hot summer's day in **1977**, in Pembrokeshire, Wales, locals reported seeing silvery objects flying through the sky, and then a **cigar-shaped UFO** landed in a field next to Broad Haven Primary School. Fourteen children saw 'small grey men in shiny suits' alight and insert something that looked like a **cattle prod** into the ground. The children were separated and told to draw what they'd seen. When the drawings were compared, they all looked identical.

Other strange things have happened in this area known as the Pembrokeshire Triangle. These included:

1. **Balls of light** followed farm vehicles and herds of cattle were 'teleported' from one field to another at Lodge Farm, home of Garel and Susan Williams.

2. Boat and aircraft **radio instruments** were interrupted across an area south of Manorbier Beach.

3. A swarm of **ladybirds** blackened out the skies.

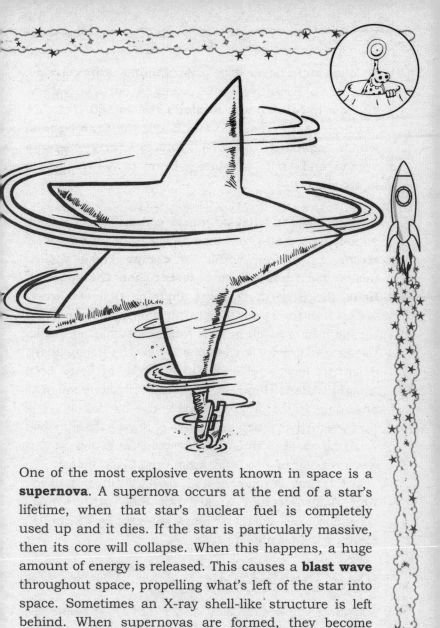

One of the most explosive events known in space is a **supernova**. A supernova occurs at the end of a star's lifetime, when that star's nuclear fuel is completely used up and it dies. If the star is particularly massive, then its core will collapse. When this happens, a huge amount of energy is released. This causes a **blast wave** throughout space, propelling what's left of the star into space. Sometimes an X-ray shell-like structure is left behind. When supernovas are formed, they become rapidly rotating '**neutron**' stars or **pulsars**. A pulsar is a neutron star that spins fast enough to give off a pulse of radio waves.

Many supernovae have been seen in nearby galaxies, but they are relatively rare events in our own galaxy. The last to be seen was **Kepler's star** in 1604.

The pulsating neutron star called the **Crab Nebula**, which exploded in 1054, rotates thirty times a second and emits a rotating beam of X-rays (like a lighthouse).

A **black hole** is what scientists call an object – such as a collapsed star or dense pulsar – with a massively strong gravitational pull. To **escape** being sucked inside, you'd have to travel **faster than the speed of light**. Since we don't know anything that can travel faster than the speed of light, that means nothing can escape from a black hole! If you did get sucked inside, the force of gravity is so strong, it would pull you apart. Scientists have a term for this – they'd say you'd been '**spaghettified**'! However, if you are unlucky enough to be caught in the pull of a super-huge black hole – one that weighed as much as billions of Suns – then instead you'd be **roasted** by super-hot plasma. Either way, it wouldn't be fun – so, stay away from black holes!

A German astronomer and maths brainbox named **Karl Schwarzschild** worked out that Earth would become a black hole if its mass was squeezed until its radius was just nine mm.

The Dark Side

Scientists still wonder why 95 per cent of the universe's mass seems to be **invisible**. They know it's all to do with types of 'dark matter' – that is, particles in space that don't emit light or radiation, and therefore can't easily

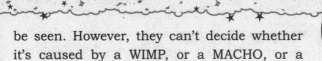

be seen. However, they can't decide whether it's caused by a WIMP, or a MACHO, or a combination of the pair.

Quickie Quiz

As you'd expect from their names, MACHOs are bigger than WIMPs. But what do WIMPs or MACHOs mean, exactly?

Do WIMPs stand for:
a) Weasle-like Imitations of Mutant Pasta?
b) Winking Inky Molecule Pieces?
c) Weakly Interacting Massive Particles?

And do MACHOs stand for:

a) **MAssive Compact Halo Objects?**
b) **MArshmallow Cookies, Highly Over-cooked?**
c) **MAnhole Covered Household Ornaments?**

Both WIMPs and MACHOs use initial letters to describe what they are. WIMP stands for Weakly Interacting Massive Particles. MACHO stands for MAssive Compact Halo Objects.

WIMPs don't interact with other objects but probably make up much of the dark matter in the universe. However, a MACHO is a 'halo' of everyday matter from the galaxies. This matter happens to be dark and therefore invisible, and includes burned-out dark stars, stray planets and other large, heavy, but dark clumps of common everyday matter. Both such objects would be invisible to telescopes.

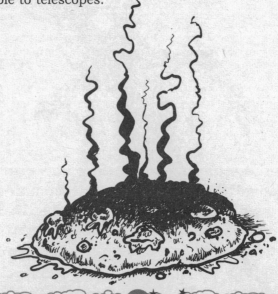

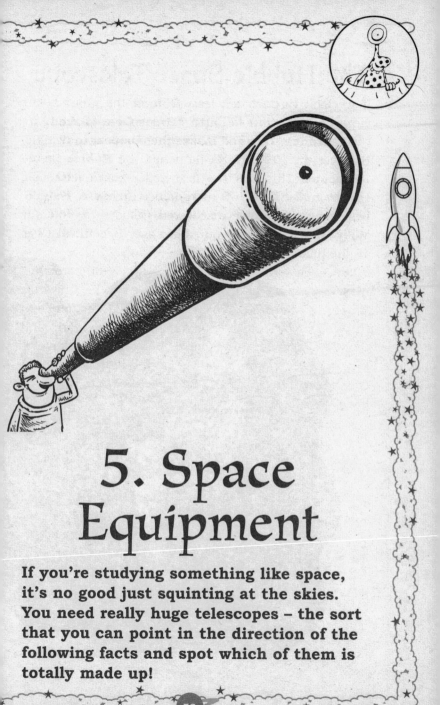

5. Space Equipment

If you're studying something like space, it's no good just squinting at the skies. You need really huge telescopes – the sort that you can point in the direction of the following facts and spot which of them is totally made up!

The Hubble Space Telescope

If we look through a telescope from the ground, our view is all fuzzy due to Earth's atmosphere, which blurs the light from stars and makes them appear to twinkle. However, in **1990**, NASA launched the **Hubble Space Telescope**. This was the first space-based telescope, and is named after US astronomer **Edwin P. Hubble**. Last century, Hubble discovered galaxies beyond our Milky Way and worked out that space is getting bigger all the time.

The Hubble Space Telescope is a tubular-shaped spacecraft and looks like it has wings, due to two 6.6 m solar panels, which collect light from the Sun to help power the spacecraft's instruments.

The telescope is the **size of a bus**, measuring 13.3 m long, and weighing more than 11,000 kg. Its main mirror – which, being located in space, allows the telescope to take sharp pictures of far-away objects – is 2.4 m wide and the telescope circles the Earth every ninety minutes. Since the Hubble Space Telescope was launched in 1990, it has sent back to Earth some 700,000 incredible pictures of the **cosmos**. These include black holes, distant planets and the giant gas clouds which create new stars. It can spot objects an incredible 12 billion light years away.

Spacesuits

Astronauts have to wear **spacesuits** so they can survive the extremes of space. There is no **atmospheric pressure** or **oxygen** in space, and a spacesuit regulates and controls conditions in a similar way to a space-shuttle cabin.

A typical astronaut's spacesuit weighs approximately **127 kg**. Of course, in the zero-gravity, weightless conditions of space, it weighs virtually nothing.

Five Good Reasons for Astronauts to Wear Spacesuits

1. To **regulate the body's temperature** and prevent it from boiling and freezing. There are huge changes in temperature in space, ranging from the super-hot 120 degrees Celsius when facing sunlight to the ultra-low temperature of -100 degrees Celsius in the shade. Fans, water-cooling systems and heat exchangers are used to maintain pressure to keep body fluids in a liquid state.

2. To provide **breathable air**. Spacesuits supply pure oxygen for breathing, rather like the supplies used by mountain climbers. Lithium hydroxide canisters remove the build-up of carbon dioxide.

3. To provide **protection** from being hit by small particles of dust or rock moving at high speeds (**micrometeoroids**), or orbiting debris from satellites or spacecraft.

4. To shield themselves from the **Sun's radiation**. In space, there is no ozone layer like we have on Earth, to reduce infrared rays.

5. To stay in **communication** with fellow astronauts or ground control. Chest- and backpacks contain radio systems.

Sometimes robotic missions don't run smoothly. On a **1982** mission to land on **Venus**, although the Russian *Venera 13* craft successfully touched down and sent readings back, for *Venera 14* it was a different matter. Unfortunately, a **camera lens cap** popped off and

landed right underneath sampling equipment. Instead of transmitting reports on what the planet Venus was made of, as intended, the spacecraft merely reported back to Earth on pictures of a discarded camera lens cap.

Astronauts working outside America's international space shuttle move around courtesy of a **MMU** – a Manned Manoeuvring Unit, which is the world's **smallest manned spacecraft**, weighing just 109 kg. The MMU is basically a chair operated by a joystick, which allows the astronaut to move freely in space and change direction by a burst of nitrogen gas. It's just 1.24 m high, 0.83 m

wide, and 1.12 m deep. It was first used in **February 1984**, on shuttle mission *STS-41-B*, when astronaut **Bruce McCandless** travelled up to 100 m away from the *Challenger* craft.

Another NASA invention is the **SAFER** – or Simplified Aid for Extravehicular Activity Rescue. This is a nitrogen gas-propelled unit that fits on astronauts' backpacks, allowing them to return to a space shuttle or station.

Astronauts aboard a space shuttle have found the perfect way to combat the **boredom** of a long journey across space. They've insisted that NASA equip the vessel with a **large multiplex cinema**, and a choice of different full-length movies. Films shown to space travellers have included *Deep Impact*, *War of the Worlds* and the six *Star Wars* movies.

America's **Saturn V rocket** was the world's **largest and most powerful rocket**, built by NASA with the sole purpose of sending astronauts to the Moon. First launched in **1967** and used on the *Apollo 11* mission, it was a massive 110.6 m high, bigger than a **thirty-six-storey building** with the *Apollo* spacecraft perched on top. It weighed 2,903 tonnes when it was standing on the launch pad.

Marshall Space Flight Centre in Alabama, USA, has been testing a device intended for the international space station that would simply **recycle** astronauts' **sweat, respiration** and even **urine** into **drinking water**

purer than any found in a tap. This water system is as large as two refrigerators. However, smaller and simpler versions are being tested on Earth.

In recent years, NASA has changed its space plans. Instead of large, expensive missions, such as sending astronauts to walk on the Moon, it now launches much smaller exploratory space trips and much more frequently than before. One such mission involves the **MESSENGER** craft. It's a name that stands for **ME**rcury **S**urface, **S**pace **EN**vironment, **GE**ochemistry, and **R**anging. Launched in 2004, MESSENGER is currently on track to orbit Mercury in 2011 and beam back the first images of Mercury in 30 years. No astronauts are on board the spacecraft.

The MESSENGER craft hopes to find the answers to the following questions:

1. Why is Mercury so dense?
2. What is the history of the rocks that make up Mercury?
3. What is Mercury's core made from?
4. What makes up Mercury's magnetic field?
5. What unusual materials are found at Mercury's poles?
6. What gases evaporate easily on Mercury's surface?

6. Meteors, Asteroids and Comets

We know there is a lot of stuff floating around in space. But what is the difference between a meteor and a meteorite? You'll know about them all once you read this next bit. And you'll remember to Find That Fib . . . won't you?

Amazing Asteroids

An **asteroid** is a large lump of rock that moves around in our solar system. They vary in size, but some asteroids can be nearly 1,000 km across.

Asteroids orbit close to the Sun and some have been captured by the gravity of planets like Earth, Mars and Jupiter. However, they are too small to be classified as planets. Known as '**minor planets**', tens of thousands of asteroids congregate in the so-called main **asteroid belt**: a vast, doughnut-shaped ring located between the orbits of Mars and Jupiter. This asteroid belt marks the junction between the inner and outer solar system and houses 90–95 per cent of all asteroids.

Because of their small size, asteroids have a low centre of gravity and so most aren't spherical like planets, but **oddly shaped**. Smaller ones are angular and shaped like potatoes and peanuts. The oddest-looking asteroid so far is called '**Kleopatra**', which looks like a 220-km-long dog bone.

Just as the Moon revolves around the Earth, some asteroids have others moving around them. Though it's only about 56 km in diameter, asteroid **Ida** has its own moon – a tiny body only one km in size. Other asteroids may well have moons of their own just waiting to be discovered.

In **January 1994**, thirty-four people reported that a bright, luminous object crossed the skies above **Santiago de Compostela**, Spain. An asteroid had blasted up to 200 cu. m of soil out of the ground, thrown trees 100 m through the air, and left behind a 29 m crater in the nearby village of Cando.

The **largest asteroid** ever found was in 1878, and was more than 1,100 km across, but weighing a mere 8 kg. The **Asteroid Peregrine** is named after its discoverer, British scientist **Dr Peregrine Cadwallader**. Asteroid Peregrine is made of a unique rock called pergrinium – similar to polystyrene foam. This rock is incredibly light due to air bubbles in its structure.

Quickie Quiz
What links Lennon and McCartney, Karl Marx, and Mark Twain? Are they:

a) all former members of The Beatles?
b) the most popular names that owners call their dogs?
c) the actual names of asteroids?

It's c). They're all names of asteroids. Originally, it seems asteroid names were originally taken from gods and goddesses, but these ran out long ago.

Nowadays, there are asteroids called Spock (as in the pointy-eared one from *Star Trek*), Edna, Bertha, Geranium, Petunia, Chicago, Granule, Requiem, Lucifer, Tolkien, Echo, Dali, Piccolo, Zulu, Limpopo, Bach, Chaucer, Nemo, Smiley, Rumpelstiltzskin, Evita, Retsina and Fanny.

On **23 March 1989**, an asteroid 400 m wide came within 640,000 km of planet Earth. This may seem a fair distance away, but scientists estimated that the asteroid, weighing 50 million tons and travelling at 74,000 km per hour, missed colliding with Earth by a mere **six hours**.

Curious Comets

A **comet** is basically a **dirty snowball** – but on a much larger scale. It's quite fragile, and composed mostly of a mixture of **ice**, **dust**, **carbon** and **silicon**. These icy bodies travel from the edge of the solar system and we can only see them when – due to the Sun's heat – clouds of gas evaporate from them and reflect light.

Comets have three distinct parts. There's a solid core called a **nucleus**. There's the **coma**, which is the dusty cloud around the nucleus. Then there are one or more

tails that trail behind the coma when a comet sweeps close to the Sun. You'll only see the coma and tails when the comet is near the Sun. When a comet approaches the Sun, it starts to vaporize. A tail of gas forms, stretching behind a comet for millions of kilometres. Each time it passes the Sun, a comet loses some of its icy nucleus.

The word 'comet' comes from the Greek word *kometes*, which means 'long haired'.

Comets **originate** from two regions, the **Kuiper Belt** and the **Oort Cloud**. The **Kuiper Belt** is the name given to the icy bodies that extend from Neptune out beyond Pluto. Comets from this region are called 'short-period comets', due to the relatively short time they take to orbit the Sun.

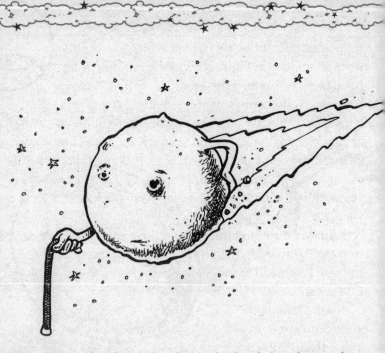

The Oort cloud is a spherical cloud in shape that surrounds the solar system. It contains an estimated **10 trillion comets** (that's a 1 followed by a whopping 13 zeros!) with the combined mass of the Earth. This is the main home for comets, 9 trillion km from the Sun. Objects from this area are the source of 'long-period comets'. They are called this because they take such a long time to orbit the Sun.

Halley's Comet

If you're lucky enough to discover a comet, it's named after you. **Edmond Halley** was an English astronomer and mathematician in the eighteenth century who mapped out the orbits of twenty-four comets that had been observed from 1337 to 1698. He showed that the

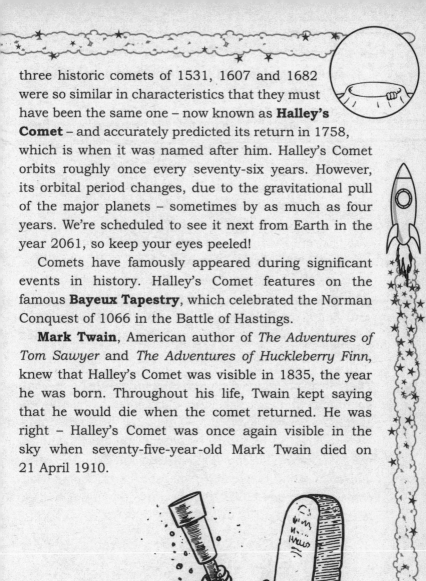

three historic comets of 1531, 1607 and 1682 were so similar in characteristics that they must have been the same one – now known as **Halley's Comet** – and accurately predicted its return in 1758, which is when it was named after him. Halley's Comet orbits roughly once every seventy-six years. However, its orbital period changes, due to the gravitational pull of the major planets – sometimes by as much as four years. We're scheduled to see it next from Earth in the year 2061, so keep your eyes peeled!

Comets have famously appeared during significant events in history. Halley's Comet features on the famous **Bayeux Tapestry**, which celebrated the Norman Conquest of 1066 in the Battle of Hastings.

Mark Twain, American author of *The Adventures of Tom Sawyer* and *The Adventures of Huckleberry Finn*, knew that Halley's Comet was visible in 1835, the year he was born. Throughout his life, Twain kept saying that he would die when the comet returned. He was right – Halley's Comet was once again visible in the sky when seventy-five-year-old Mark Twain died on 21 April 1910.

Comets are also said to have accompanied the deaths of:

Charlemagne (AD 814)
Attila the Hun (AD 453)
Emperor Valentinian III (AD 455)

And they appeared during the Great Fire of London (1666) and the birth of Napoleon (1769).

The European Space Agency's probe, **Giotto**, took **pictures** of **Halley's Comet** in **1986** – the last time it was sighted. These showed that it was a bit potato-like in shape, measured about 16 km long, 8 km wide, and had a rough surface covered with what looked like craters and hills. The gases it burnt off as it travelled across the sky were largely water vapour from its icy core. This core is then surrounded by a halo of gases.

Giotto had been named after the fourteenth-century Italian painter, who had included Halley's Comet as the Star of Bethlehem in his famous painting *Adoration Of The Magi*. That's because Giotto had been impressed when he saw Halley's Comet pass by in 1301.

The Hale-Bopp Comet

On **23 July 1995**, at the same time but in different places, two American astronomers, **Alan Hale** and **Thomas Bopp**, spotted an unusually bright comet outside of Jupiter's orbit. So, what did they do?

a) **had a corned-beef sandwich and admired the sight?**

b) **hid under their chairs, petrified?**

c) **contacted the Central Bureau for Astronomical Telegrams?**

The answer's c). They contacted the Central Bureau for Astronomical Telegrams in Cambridge, Massachusets, and reported their discovery. Traditionally, when a comet is first sighted, it is named after the person who discovered it. In this case, Alan and Thomas shared the honour between them!

This new comet was named **Comet Hale-Bopp**. It's the most distant comet ever discovered by amateur comet observers, and it appeared 1,000 times brighter than Halley's Comet did at the same distance.

Mighty Meteoroids, Meteors and Meteorites

A **meteoroid** is generally smaller than an asteroid, being an interplanetary chunk of matter whizzing through space, ranging from mere millimetres up to a kilometre in length. Meteoroids are thought to be the debris from asteroids and comets.

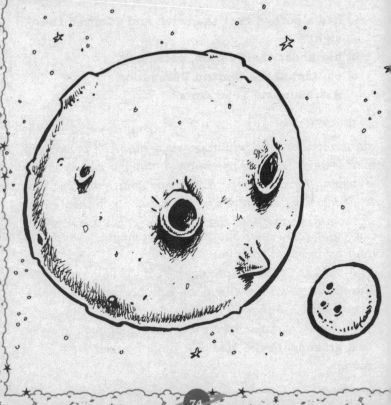

A **meteor** is what we call the **flash of light** we see in the night sky when a meteoroid smashes through our atmosphere. A meteor is also known as a shooting star, and you may have been lucky enough to see one. Meteors **heat up** on entering the Earth's atmosphere and travel at speeds of up to 100,000 km per hour. Most meteors are so small that they get completely vaporized, and never reach the planet's surface.

If any part of a meteoroid survives the fall through the atmosphere and actually does land on Earth, it's called a **meteorite**. Although most meteorites are very small, their size can range from pebble-sized (about a fraction of a gramme) to the size of a huge boulder (100 kg or more).

On 12 July 1998, a Canadian golfer was playing a round on the Doon Valley Golf Course near **Kitchener, Ontario**. He was amazed to find a 203 g meteorite sizzling on the golf link, and was rewarded for his find by the golf club offering him free membership for a whole year.

However, he wasn't half as lucky as his fellow golfer, who narrowly missed getting killed by the falling meteor as he stood on the sixth hole.

Every couple of hundred thousand years or so, huge meteorites do tend to smash into the Earth's surface, creating huge craters on impact.

The best-preserved of these is **Meteor Crater** in Arizona's arid desert, which was formed around 50,000 years ago. It's 175 m deep and 1.3 km wide.

7. Famous Firsts

When the two great super powers of the USA and the the former Soviet Union became determined to be the first to put humans on the Moon, it was known as the great Space Race. Can you Find That Fib amongst these firsts?

1957

The world's **first man-made satellite** was sent into space by the former Soviet Union. Record-breaking *Sputnik 1* was a round sphere resembling a very large basketball. Weighing 83 kg, it was only 58 cm across. *Sputnik 1* took about ninety-eight minutes to orbit the Earth. The launch of *Sputnik 1* marked the dawn of the Space Age.

1957

A few months later, **Laika the dog** was the **first living creature** to orbit Earth, launched aboard *Sputnik 2*. The animal had been a stray dog, living on Moscow's streets before being captured and blasted off into space.

1958

The **first monkey** was sent into space. **Gordo** the monkey was the first living creature the USA had launched into space.

1959

The USSR sent the **first unmanned space probe to the Moon**. *Lunik 2* took thirty-six hours to reach the Moon, but it did not return.

1961

The **first human in space** was **Yuri Gagarin**, but he wasn't the Russian space programme's first choice of cosmonaut. It was the unlucky Boris Pulitov. Due to technical problems, Boris waited for thirteen hours for the rocket to blast into space. Fifteen minutes before lift-off, Boris had to race to the rocket's on-board toilet. Unfortunately for Boris, the locking mechanism seized, trapping him inside. The Russians abandoned the space flight with minutes to go. They also hushed up the whole incident, and instead took second-choice cosmonaut, Yuri Gagarin, up into space the next day.

1963

Valentina Tereshkova was the **first woman in space**. She flew on Russian spacecraft *Vostok 6* and spent almost three days in orbit. The main purpose of her mission was to find out how space flight affected males and females. Valentina also had to communicate with a second orbiting vehicle, *Vostok 5*, flown by cosmonaut Valeri Bykovsky.

1962, 1998

American war hero **John Glenn** holds two different 'firsts' in the US space programme. He was the **first American to orbit the Earth**. On 20 February 1962, Glenn piloted the *Mercury-Atlas 6 Friendship 7* spacecraft. Launched from Kennedy Space Center, Florida, he completed a successful three-orbit mission around the Earth, in four hours, fifty-five minutes and twenty-three seconds.

John Glenn was also the **first septugenerian** in space. On 29 October 1998, NASA launched the space shuttle *Discovery* mission *STS-95* with a seventy-seven-year-old Glenn on board. Glenn spent nine days in space undergoing various experiments to research possible links between the human ageing process and the ways in which being weightless for long periods of time affects astronauts. *Discovery* returned to Earth successfully on 7 November 1998. This was thirty-six years and eight months after Glenn had first orbited the Earth.

1965

Know what extra-vehicular activity means to space scientists? It's walking in space – and is referred to as EVA for short. On 18 March 1965 **Alexei Arkhipovich Leonov** was the **first person to go spacewalking** when he left Russia's *Voskhod 2* to carry out repairs on the spacecraft. His 'walk' lasted for about ten minutes.

1968:
Quickie Quiz

As _Apollo 8_ headed for the Moon, its astronauts were the first humans to look out of their craft and see . . . well, what did they see? Was it:

a) A black hole?

b) An alien spacecraft taking a close look at them?

c) Planet Earth from space?

The answer's c). The astronauts were treated to the first view of planet Earth from space.

1969

The **first person on the Moon** was **Neil Armstrong**, command pilot of the _Apollo 11_ mission. He took his 'small step for man, giant leap for mankind' at 02:56:15 GMT on 21 July 1969. He was followed by Col. Edwin Eugene Aldrin, Jr – known to everyone as 'Buzz'. Pilot Lt-Col. Michael Collins didn't get a chance to Moonwalk – he was left orbiting above them in the command module.

1970

The USSR sent the **first unmanned robotic probe**, *Luna 16*, to **land on the Moon** and return to Earth. It landed in the **Sea of Fertility**, and collected a 101 g sample of Moon rock.

1986

Russia's *Mir* space station was the world's **first permanent residence in space**. It was occupied by cosmonauts almost continuously from 1986 to 1999, and crew lived and worked within the cramped conditions of the 13 m long and 4 m wide core section of the craft. In 1993, the Russians and the Americans began to cooperate with one another on space projects. *Mir* was the first project to benefit from this shared knowledge.

1991

Helen Sharman became **Britain's first astronaut**. She'd applied to an advert which said: 'Astronaut wanted. No experience necessary.' She was selected from over 13,000 applicants to be the UK's representative on the Russian space mission, Project Juno. When she blasted off into space, she carried with her a photograph of the Queen, a butterfly brooch her dad had given her, and a space passport in case her spacecraft was forced to land outside the Soviet Union. Helen spent about eight days in space, flying aboard Russia's *Soyuz TM-12* spacecraft. And what was Helen's previous job? She was an engineer at the chocolate firm which make Mars bars!

1997

The **first space funeral** took place when an aircraft carrying a modified *Pegasus* rocket was launched into

Earth orbit. The rocket carried the ashes of twenty-four space pioneers and enthusiasts, at a cost of almost £3,000 each. They included the remains of **Gene Roddenberry**, famous for creating TV's *Star Trek*.

However, if we are to believe the gossip, Roddenberry had technically already been in space. It seems that an astronaut and friend of the *Star Trek* creator had secretly stowed a few grams of his ashes on board a space-shuttle mission in 1992.

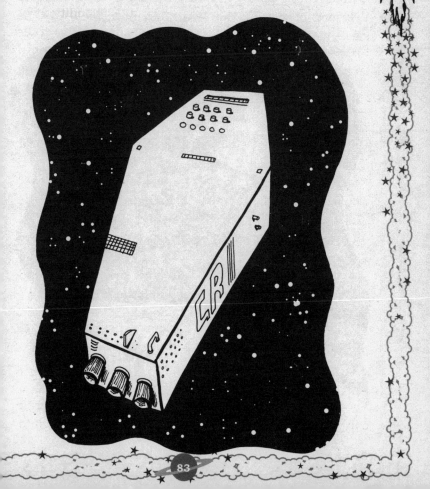

1999

A few years later, the **first space burial** on the Moon took place on 31 July 1999. That's when the US Moon probe *Luna Prospector* completed its observation from the Moon's orbit as it plunged into a crater on its surface. The probe carried a small, lipstick-shaped container holding 28 g of the ashes of astronomer **Dr Eugene Shoemaker**, who'd died in 1997. This was the first time that ashes were taken to an astral body, as a final resting place. When he was alive, Dr Shoemaker dreamed of visiting the Moon and now, in a way, he has!

2001

Forty years after the first man was sent into orbit, an American businessman named **Dennis Tito** became the world's **first space tourist**. He reportedly paid Russia $20 million (£14 million) to visit the international space station (ISS) for seven days from 28 April to 6 May 2001. He arrived aboard a Russian *Soyuz* spacecraft, to the dismay of NASA, who initially objected to having a space tourist aboard the internationally funded ISS. NASA changed their mind after Tito signed agreements which stated he wouldn't sue NASA in the event of injury or death. He also agreed to pay for anything he broke aboard the station, and was not allowed to visit any American sections of the station unaccompanied.

8. Astronaut Antics

Have you ever thought of becoming an astronaut? All you have to do is write to:

Astronaut Selection Office
NASA Johnson Space Center
Houston, TX 77058
United States of America

Nevertheless, you also need to be adult, physically very fit, have 1,000 hours experience flying a jet aircraft, and you need to know a bit about space – the sort that'll enable you to Find That Fib!

The USA calls anyone who travels more than 80 km (50 miles) above the Earth an '**astronaut**'. Russia (when it was known as the Soviet Union) prefer to call a space-traveller a '**cosmonaut**'. This comes from the Greek words *kosmos* for 'universe' and *nautes* for 'sailor'.

Neil Armstrong may be extraordinary because he's the first man to walk on the Moon, but every so often he needs something as ordinary as a **haircut**. However, Armstrong's monthly haircut earned barber Mark Sizemore £1,600. That's because a thrifty Sizemore sold Armstrong's hair clippings to a collector who already owns hair trimmings from Elvis Presley, Charles Dickens and John F. Kennedy. Armstrong demanded Sizemore donate his cut of the money to charity or get the trimmings back. However, the barber refused, leaving an angry Armstrong feeling anything but over the moon!

President Richard Nixon was so overjoyed that First Man On The Moon Neil Armstrong was American, that he passed a law in the American Congress that Armstrong should be given the name of '**Moonman**'. Neil 'Moonman' Armstrong was, however, unhappy with his new nickname and never used it. Privately, he felt that an astronaut with the nickname 'Buzz' – as everyone called his co-Moonwalker Buzz Aldrin – was a far cooler nickname.

Russian cosmonaut **Dr Valeri Polyakov** set a manned space-flight record by making the **single longest space flight**. That was when he spent over a year aboard *Mir LD-4*, launched on **8 January 1994**. The doctor spent **437.7 days in space**, during which time he was part of three crews sent as part of Russia's *Soyuz* space programme. Dr Polyakov took blood samples and performed other medical experiments in space, as research for future manned space flights to Mars.

Quickie Quiz

Texas is the only US state that permits astronaut-loving residents to:

a) Have a wee in space?

b) Vote in space?

c) Ride a bicycle in space without a helmet?

The answer's b). Texas residents can cast absentee votes from space. Astronaut David Wolf was the first Texan to do this, when he cast his vote for the Houston major via an email transmitted from Russia's Mir space station in 1997.

Since space flights began, only **434 people** have flown in orbit above the Earth. See the list below for which city to be born in, if you want to be an astronaut.

Top Ten Cities Where Astronauts Were Born

Birthplace	Number of astronauts produced
1. Moscow, Russia	40
2. Boston, USA	9
3. Chicago, USA	8
4. Cleveland, USA	8
5. New York, USA	8
6. Leningrad, Russia	8
7. Philadelphia, USA	7
8. Los Angeles, USA	5
9. Washington, USA	5
10. Springfield, USA	5

9. Living in Space

Have you ever wondered what it would be like to live, eat and sleep in the weightlessness of space? Well, wonder no longer because the next chapter will reveal all. But don't forget to Find That Fib!

When completed, the **international space station** will be four times the size of the late Russian *Mir* space station – measuring 109 m across and 88 m long, with solar panels covering 4,050 sq. m. The internal volume of the space station will be about as big as the inside of a Boeing 747 passenger airline cabin.

Ten Things Astronauts Can Take On-board the International Space Station

1. Comb
2. Pair of scissors
3. Toothbrush and toothpaste
4. Soap
5. Shampoo
6. Towels
7. Tissues
8. Velcro kit-bag to attach to wall, and prevent it floating away
9. Shaving kit (for men)
10. Make-up (for women)

The pressures of space can make certain materials react strangely. In 1957, cosmonaut **Vito Slobadarnov** tested out a new type of spacesuit, made from **silk** produced by a rare **spider** found only in the Russian Ural Mountains. Unfortunately, Vito's natural body oils reacted with the garment and caused it to split, after only twelve hours in space. The spacesuit fell to pieces soon after, and poor Vito had to quickly change into a back-up suit constructed from man-made fibres.

What do astronauts have to use to *shave* in space?

a) Ice-cold water and heated up towels.
b) Shaving lotion made of crushed Moon rock.
c) Special razors that suck in stray whiskers.

The answer's c). Stray whiskers floating around in the weightless conditions of a space capsule or station would cause havoc if even one got into shuttle controls.

Eating and Drinking in Space

Being weightless in space affects astronauts' **taste buds** and **sense of smell**. That's why astronauts in orbit always prefer food to be covered in salt, pepper and other spices so that they can taste them.

When astronauts get peckish, they can tuck into foods served hot or cold, and from a choice of around seventy-two different food items. Eating in space has come a long way since the 1960s when astronauts ate just cubes of food and freeze-dried powders that had to be made tasty by adding water. Nowadays, food is eaten directly from flexible containers using ordinary knives, forks and spoons. These food containers are attached to a meal tray which is, in turn, attached to an astronaut's lap. Drinks are drunk using a squeezy bottle like today's sport bottles.

Although it's been more than twenty years since man made the last trip to the Moon, you can still buy the **freeze-dried ice cream** that astronauts on the *Apollo* space programme ate while travelling through space. Freeze-dried foods were specially developed by NASA to be eaten by astronauts under conditions of weightlessness in space.

Quickie Quiz

Ice cream is frozen to a blisteringly cold -40 degrees Celsius. It's then vacuum dried and placed in a special foil pouch. What flavour was this? Was it:

a) Neopolitan?
b) Neoprene rubber?
c) Neoprene rubber with crunchy nuts and raspberry sauce?

The answer's a). The freeze-dried flavour was Neopolitan – a scrummy mix of vanilla, strawberry and chocolate. And the taste was – as you'd expect – out of this world!

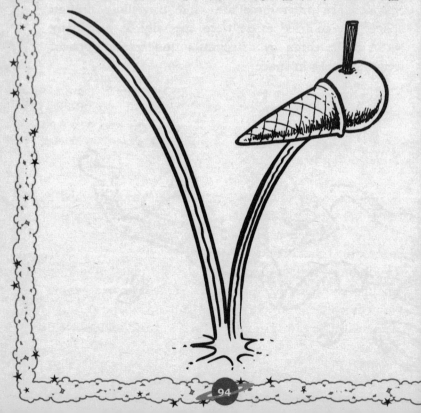

Keeping Clean

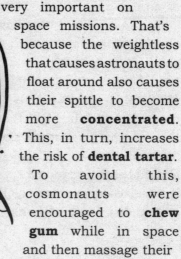

Cleaning teeth is very important on space missions. That's because the weightless that causes astronauts to float around also causes their spittle to become more **concentrated**. This, in turn, increases the risk of **dental tartar**. To avoid this, cosmonauts were encouraged to **chew gum** while in space and then massage their gums with a rubber finger sleeve after each meal.

People **sweat** much more in space than they do on Earth. On average, cosmonauts lose about 1 kg of sweat for every six hours of spacewalking. On Earth, we lose about 600 g of sweat in a day.

It wasn't easy keeping clean on-board early space missions. Not only were conditions cramped, but water behaves strangely in space. It can split, forming walnut-sized drops that stick to the skin and – under weightless conditions – it floats around freely in droplets. Because of this, shower water had to be sprayed into a **sealed shower cabin**, and astronauts had to breathe through a special tube put through the wall of the cabin to avoid choking.

Because preparing the cabin for showers took as long as the act of bathing itself, the crew members of the seventh mission to *Mir* – in 1990 – threw the shower cabin into space.

The alternative to showering in space is much simpler. Cosmonaut Valeri Polyakov, who completed a space flight that lasted 437 days, used **wet towels** to keep himself clean, claiming that he found them very effective. He even said his skin and hair were in better condition after the flight than before. Bill Shepherd, the first international space station crew commander, also likes using wet towels to keep clean in space. Even today, aboard the international space station, astronauts wash themselves all over with cloths that have been dipped in special disinfectant lotions.

Going to the Toilet

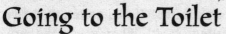

How do astronauts go to the toilet? Well, modern astronauts use a toilet with a **strong vacuum** pull that makes sure bits of . . . well, poo . . . don't float around the cabin!

As that vacuum's so strong, astronauts have to buckle up – using specially strengthened belts on their thighs – before they sit down to do their business . . . otherwise that strong vacuum might suck them out too!

On *Apollo 13*, astronauts **peed** into little **bags** and pushed liquid 'presents' through an airlock to float around space! They also used to refer to the act of peeing as 'visiting the constellation U-ri-ine'.

The **Endeavor** space shuttle has a **toilet** that cost over **12 million pounds** to build. When you're in there, all the poo slides into a series of canisters, with cleverly locking lids, ready for disposal. This must make it the world's most expensive toilet!

Astronaut's Checklist Before Going on a Spacewalk
1. Spacesuit with 12-part multi-layered structure.
2. Boots.
3. Gloves.
4. Primary life-support system (PLSS) worn on the back, to feed oxygen supplies.
5. Display and control module on the chest.
6. EMU – or 'extra-vehicular mobility unit'. This has subsystems that interconnect in single-handed operation for either normal or emergency use.

The EMU includes:

a) urine-collection and storage device

b) liquid cooling and ventilation garment

c) one-piece water-cooled, ventilated Spandex undergarment

d) in-suit drink bag containing 595 g of water

e) 'Snoopy Cap' or 'Communications Carrier Assembly' which are made up of headphones and microphones for two-way communications.

Sleeping in Space

This is quite different from sleeping on Earth. Instead of a bed, you have a wall-mounted **sleeping bag** that you slip into and zip up. The bag is equipped with **arm restraints** to prevent your arms from floating above your head while you sleep.

Astronauts working aboard the international space station sleep in **two small crew cabins**, each just big enough for one person to lie down inside a sleeping bag. At present, three astronauts live and work in space for months at a time. So, where does that third astronaut sleep? Well, he or she can sleep anywhere in the space station so long as the astronaut attaches themselves to something to prevent them from floating around.

Five Handy Inventions That Were Originally Invented for Use in Space

1. Bar-coding
2. Thermal imaging
3. Ear thermometers
4. Ski boots
5. Edible toothpaste

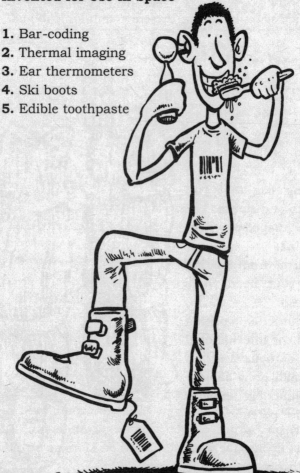

10.
Space-age Stars of TV and Film

For years, we've enjoyed watching films and TV shows which are based in space. It's what we call science fiction, or sci-fi for short. So, can you Find That Fib amongst these questions about space stars?

Captain Scarlet and his colourful colleagues work for an organization called **Spectrum**. To help them in their work, they sometimes use a nuclear powered pogo-stick device called a BOUNCE – short for 'Biometric Observational Undercover Nuclear-powered Cruising Equipment'. A BOUNCE is ideal for allowing Spectrum agents to quickly reach dangerous situations, especially on rough, rocky landscapes.

Spectrum's Martian foes, the **Mysterons**, were kept invisible on purpose by creator Gerry Anderson. That was just in case life was ever found on Mars as he didn't want his Mysterons to look 'wrong'.

Quickie Quiz

Who were the only actors (and not the characters) to have appeared in all six *Star Wars* films? Were they:

a) Ewan McGregor and Harrison Ford?

b) Paul and Barry Chuckle, the Chuckle Brothers?

c) Anthony Daniels and Kenny Baker?

The answer's c). Anthony Daniels and Kenny Baker played everyone's favourite mechanical double act, C-3PO and R2-D2.

Darth Vader was recently voted the **Greatest Screen Villain of All Time**.

Other notable baddies from outer space
- *Dr Who*'s **Daleks** plus the new villains, the **Slitheens**
- The **Martian invaders** from *War of the Worlds*
  Star Trek's **Klingons**

Yoda, the most senior member of **Jedi High Council** on Coruscant, is well over **900** years old. His final Jedi Knight apprentice was Anakin Skywalker's son, Luke.

You may have seen TV's **Dr Who** travelling around in an old police box called a **TARDIS**. These initials stand for 'Time and Relative Dimension in Space'. The spin-off series starring the Doctor's time-travelling pal, **Captain Jack**, is called **Torchwood**, which is a jumbling up of the letters in 'Doctor Who'.

When the **Daleks** from *Dr Who* were built in 1963, there wasn't enough money to build all six Daleks listed in the script. Producers could only afford four, so they had to use two cardboard cut-outs with photos of the Daleks pasted on them to make it look like there were all six Daleks in a scene.

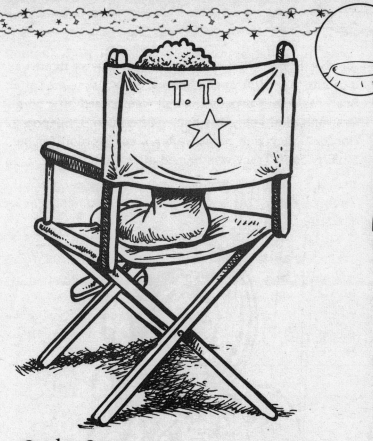

Quickie Quiz

In which Steven Spielberg space blockbuster movie was the lead role played by the world's smallest actress – 2 ft 7 in. tall Tamara de Treaux? Was it:

a) *ET – The Extra Terrestrial?*
b) *Deep Impact?*
c) *Men In Black?*

The answer's a). Tiny Tamara played ET in shots where Steven Spielberg didn't use a model.

All of Jeff Tracy's boys in **Thunderbirds** were named as a tribute to real-life **space heroes**. Scott was named after Scott Malcolm Carpenter. Virgil was named after Virgil Grissom. Alan Tracy was named after Alan B. Shephard. Gordon Tracy was named after Leroy Gordon Cooper. Finally, John Tracy was named after John Glenn.

Having come from the planet **Krypton**, even a superhero like **Superman** can be stopped by a blast of Kryptonite. Superman's adventures feature a number of different types of this deadly material:

- **Green Kryptonite** quickly causes loss of strength and can eventually lead to death for any Kryptonian.
- **Blue Kryptonite** only affects creatures from the parallel planet of Bizarro, much like Green Kryptonite affects Superman on Earth.
- **Gold Kryptonite** is deadly. If Superman was exposed to Gold K, it would take away his powers forever.
- **Red Kryptonite** has various temporary effects upon people from the planet Krypton. These include, say, growing wings, or turning into a turtle.
- **White Kryptonite** kills any type of plant life.

Characters with the initials '**L. L.**' crop up all the time in Superman's life.

Lana Lang was the girlfriend of a young Clark Kent – the alter ego of Superman.

Lois Lane is, of course, the love of the adult Superman's life.

Lyla Lerrol was the blonde fellow Kryptonian that Superman almost married.

Lara Lor-van was Superman's mother's name.

Lex Luthor is Superman's worst enemy.

Ways You Can Enjoy *The Hitchhiker's Guide to the Galaxy*

- **Listen to the radio series.**
- **Watch the TV series.**
- **Read the series of books.**
- **Listen to the CD or record.**
- **Play the best-selling computer game.**
- **Go to the cinema and watch the movie.**

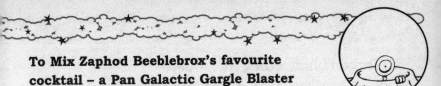

To Mix Zaphod Beeblebrox's favourite cocktail – a Pan Galactic Gargle Blaster

Take some Ol' Janx Spirit, and mix with some Santraginean seawater.

Add a slosh of Arcturan Mega-gin, and mix with some Fallian marsh gas.

Then take some Qualactin Hypermint extract, and add it to the tooth of an Algolian Suntiger, together with some Zamphuor and an olive.

Enjoy, if you can – the effect of drinking one of these, according to *The Hitchhiker's Guide to the Galaxy*, is supposedly like 'having your brains smashed out by a slice of lemon wrapped around a gold brick'!

Three Handy Klingon Phrases

Want to speak Klingon like they do in *Star Trek*? Try these out:

1. *HIjol* (pronounced *khi-JOL*) – Beam me aboard!
2. *nuqDaq yuch Dapol* (pronounced *NOOK-dak yooch da-POL*) – Where do you keep the chocolate?
3. *blmoHqu* (pronounced *bi-mokh-KOO*) – You're very ugly!

By the way, the **Starship Enterprise** in the *Star Trek* series was originally called the *SS Yorktown* in the first TV scripts.

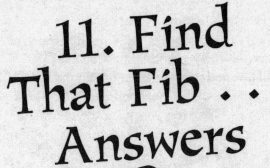

11. Find That Fib . . . Answers

Chapter 1. The Earth in Space

If you didn't believe that load of rubbish about the Dustbin Galaxy, then congratulations – you Found That Fib!

Incidentally, the nearest neighbouring galaxy to planet Earth is the Andromeda Galaxy. It is 2.2 million light years away, being the nearest major galaxy to our own Milky Way Galaxy.

Chapter 2. The Planets and Our Moon

If you didn't believe that the planet Uranus was originally intended to be called 'Tinkerbell' after a telescope-knocking pet cat, then well done – you Found That Fib!

However, Herschel did originally name it 'the Georgian planet' – or 'George' – in honour of King George III. It was later decided to follow tradition and name it as other planets had been named, using names from ancient mythology.

Chapter 3. Lost in Space

If you didn't believe that story about the *Apollo 12* astronauts spotting a lump of choccie cookie spat out by Buzz Aldrin, then congratulations, because you Found That Fib!

However, it is a fact that screwdrivers, bolts, broken pens and bent CDs are amongst the everyday stuff still floating about in outer space.

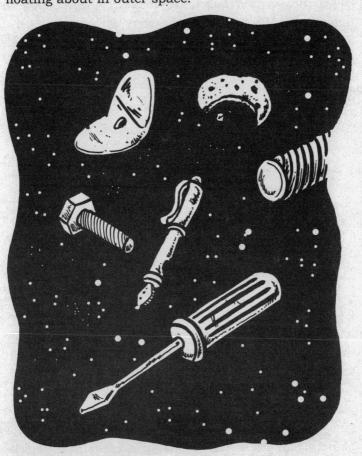

Chapter 4. Strange Space Happenings

If you disbelieved that nonsense about one of the giant stones of Stonehenge taking off like a giant spaceship, then well done – you Found That Fib!

However, it is true that in August 1994, several witnesses did claim to see a UFO fly over Salisbury Plain near Stonehenge. It apparently crashed into Boscombe Down runway and was taken to a US Airforce base in America. In March that year a lorry driver named Paul Savage reported seeing a small black triangular aircraft fire a beam of light at Stonehenge. As the area was used for testing US spy-planes, it's likely that the UFOs were actually secret aircraft prototypes.

Chapter 5. Space Equipment

If you didn't believe that story about a multiplex cinema showing films to astronauts on board the international space shuttle, then well done – you Found That Fib!

However, it's completely true that the international space station's module provides almost everything else the crew might need – personal sleeping quarters, a toilet, hygiene facilities, a kitchen, a treadmill and an exercise bicycle.

Chapter 6. Meteors, Asteroids and Comets

If you didn't believe that nonsense about the largest asteroid being the incredibly light Asteroid Peregrine, then congratulations, you Found That Fib!

However, it is true that the largest asteroid, Ceres, measures 950 km. This makes it less than a third of the size of the Moon.

Chapter 7. Famous Firsts

If you didn't believe that nonsense about Boris Pullito waiting for thirteen hours and then getting locked in th capsule toilet, then well done – you Found That Fib!

However, Ukrainian Pilot Cosmonaut Leonid K. Kadenyu actually did have a long wait for a space flight. Joining th Russian space programme in 1976, he had to wait twenty one years before he flew aboard the space shuttle *Columbi* in 1997. Fortunately, Kadenyuk didn't get locked inside an toilets during that time.

Chapter 8. Astronaut Antics

If you didn't believe that nonsense about Neil Armstrong being given such a silly name as 'Moonman', then congratulations . . . you Found That Fib!

However, it is true that Russian Cosmonaut Yuri Gagarin was often referred to as 'The Columbus of The Cosmos'.

Chapter 9. Living in Space

If you didn't believe that nonsense about Russian cosmonaut Vito Slobadarnov's special spider fibre spacesuit falling to pieces, then congrats . . . you Found That Fib!

However, it is true that in early Soviet space missions, temperatures were so hot inside a capsule that the Russian Cosmonauts would pilot their spacecraft while sitting in their pants and vests.

Chapter 10. Space-age Stars of TV and Film

If you didn't believe that nonsense about Captain Scarlet and his Spectrum agents riding on a BOUNCE – a nuclear-powered pogo stick – then well done . . . you Found That Fib!

Actually, Captain Scarlet and his fellow Spectrum members do travel in SPVs – but that is short for 'Spectrum Pursuit Vehicle'. These are modelled on the World Army Air Force 'Zeus' combat tank from the year 2064, and armed with a single ground-to-air rocket launcher. SPVs have twenty wheels and twin caterpillar tracks.

Puffin by Post

The Know-It-All Guide to Amazing Space – Nigel Crow

If you have enjoyed this book and want to read more,
then check out these other great Puffin titles.
You can order any of the following books direct with Puffin by Post:

Know-It-All Guides: Mighty Egyptians • 9780141320731	£3.99
Fab facts about pyramids, mummies and pharaohs!	

Know-It-All Guides: Conquering Romans • 9780141319728	£3.99
Impress your family, friends and teachers!	

Know-It-All Guides: Incredible Creatures • 9780141319759	£3.99
Things you never knew about the animal kingdom!	

Know-It-All Guides: Freaky Football • 9780141320717	£3.99
Become a footy wizard on and off the pitch!	

Know-It-All Guides: Heroic Greeks • 9780141320700	£3.99
Even more flabbergasting facts to sink your teeth into!	

Just contact:

Puffin Books, C/o Bookpost, PO Box 29,
Douglas, Isle of Man, IM99 1BQ
Credit cards accepted. For further details:
Telephone: 01624 677237
Fax: 01624 670923

You can email your orders to: bookshop@enterprise.net
Or order online at: www.bookpost.co.uk

Free delivery in the UK.
Overseas customers must add £2 per book.

Prices and availability are subject to change.

Visit puffin.co.uk to find out about the latest titles, read extracts and
exclusive author interviews, and enter exciting competitions.
You can also browse thousands of Puffin books online.